CONTEMPORARY LIVING

BETA-PLUS

CONTEMPORARY LIVING

January 2007
ISBN 13: 978 90 772 1377 3
ISBN 10: 90 772 1377 5

p. 2

A project by architect
Baudouin Courtens.

p. 4-5

A project by
Vlassak-Verhulst.

CONTENTS

FOREWORD

This follow-up to the bestsellers "CONTEMPORARY INTERIORS" and "CONTEM-PORARY HOUSES" is a completely new book featuring fourteen reports on contemporary homes created by renowned interior architects and designers.

Once more, the reports in this book demonstrate that contemporary living nowadays calls for more than the harmonious integration of the latest designer furniture and home technology in a modern context.

In each project, architects and interior specialists have worked to create a fascinating mix of volumes and perspective, of light and atmosphere, of materials, shapes and colours. They have designed real homes whose owners take great pleasure every day in the space that has been created.

Wim Pauwels
Publisher

p. 12-13
A project by
Bataille-ibens.

A project by Philip Simoen.

PART I

INSPIRATIONAL HOUSES

MASTERS OF
MODERN ARCHITECTURE

Since 1970, Vlassak-Verhulst has been one of Belgium's leading construction companies.

As a specialist in the construction of exclusive villas, Vlassak-Verhulst is not only known for its magnificent country houses and faithful renditions of presbytery-style homes: the company has also earned its spurs in the area of contemporary architecture and interior design.

This report about a decidedly contemporary house is a prime example of the mastery that the company displays in this field.

The brushed-oak front door has been stained in brown-black.

The exterior walls have been rendered with an unpainted, textured 'crepi' finish in a taupe/mink shade.

The south-facing wall, with its preponderance of glass, recedes within the U-shaped architectural framework. In the centre of the bangkirai terrace is a simple pool that adjoins the dining room.

The large cross window provides an accent on the rear façade: the dining room is below and the master bedroom, with its magnificent view over the garden, is above.

A cast-concrete washbasin.

The floating staircase is a real eye-catcher within the minimalist design of the entrance hall. This staircase is made from brown-black stained oak, with a stainless-steel handrail adding the finishing touch.
Five floor spots provide sophisticated illumination for the space between the stairs and the white-painted wall.

p. 24-25
Sober simplicity in the living room, with a dark-brown wall as a backdrop.

A solid-oak table on a
bleached-oak wooden
floor.

The large windows ensure plenty of light in this living room.

The central block also serves as a breakfast
bar.
The surface is in sapphire black, a thick block
with a smoothed finish.

A pale-grey Lacobel glass wall behind the
work surface, with a concealed illumination
strip.
The kitchen floor is in large (60x60 cm) Inca
Basaltina tiles.

Inca Basaltina, laid in strips, was selected for the bathroom floor.

p. 32-33

A line of concealed spotlights illuminates the glass wall that leads to the walk-in shower on one side and the toilet on the other.

The sober look of this bedroom reinforces the feeling of space and uniformity that characterises the whole house.

CONTEMPORARY LIVING ON THE SCHELDT

A young self-employed couple gave interior architect Bert Van Bogaert carte blanche to design and create a stylish, strictly minimalist loft for them with a breathtaking view of the river Scheldt.

The generous budget meant that only high-quality materials were used, and it was possible to devote attention to the finish of even the smallest details.

The loft faces south and the large windows allow in plenty of light.

The whole project was designed to be as empty and spacious as possible.

The dining table is parallel to the kitchen unit and has the same length.

p. 36
The kitchen appliances are concealed behind hinged and sliding panels. The canopy is as large as the cooking unit and has four separate ventilation grilles with a motor on the roof providing almost silent extraction. The surface, finished in natural basalt, includes a breakfast area.

To the right are the sliding doors with shelves behind; to the left is the cooking island with its separate cooking rings. The passageway leads to the relaxation space.

p. 42-43
The pivoting entrance door is made from a single piece of wood. The centrally positioned entrance hall separates the sitting room from the kitchen and dining area.

p. 44-45
Above the gas fire, a plasma screen has been built into the wall. The air-conditioning has also been incorporated into the wall and fitted with a subtle vent that runs the length of the fire. The ceiling-height windows provide a perfect view over the Scheldt from the sitting room.

p. 38
Behind the panels are the grill and the deep-fryer with their own extractor.

The basins are also made of basalt.

p. 46

Indirect floor lighting and, to the right, the way through to the two children's bedrooms, which can be closed off with the double sliding doors with handles designed by Bert Van Bogaert.

A view of the parents' bedroom area, seen from the corridor by the children's room.

The floating sink area is in basalt. The sunken bath has been clad with the same natural stone. The cupboards above have sliding mirrors.

The spacious walk-in shower is also clad with basalt and has two rain showerheads. The removable floor slabs render the drain invisible.

There is a wonderful view over the Scheldt from the bedroom.

Spacious storage cupboards with subtly incorporated air-conditioning vents in the bedroom.

The sleeping area of the children's rooms is on the same level as the work surface.

TWO CONTEMPORARY INTERIORS

Two projects by RR Interiors from Knokke are presented in this report: the interior of a woodland villa in Bruges (p. 52-57) and the complete furnishing of a holiday home in Westkapelle (p. 58-63).

Two Minotti chairs in the foreground.

To the left of the photo is a comfortable Long Island sofa by Flexform.

A Stone carpet by Bic and a Casamilano coffee table add the finishing touches to the sitting area.

Solid-oak tables from the RR Interiors workshop in the dining area and kitchen.

Casamilano chairs and a light designed by Piet Boon. Wengé shelves and sideboard by Poliform.

Built-in cupboards by Poliform and a Victor Large chair by Flexform. The shelving and console were made in the RR Interiors workshop.

These chairs from the RR Interiors workshop have been covered with a black linen material from Flexform.

Specially made cupboards and desk by Poliform.

RR Interiors opted for colour in the children's rooms.

Comfortable boxspring beds and bunk beds as a creative solution.

QUALITY OF
THE HIGHEST STANDARD

Vincent Vangheluwe has been working as a consultant in interior design and the construction sector for fifteen years.

Supervising projects at the top of the range (large farmhouses, castles, luxury apartments) has given him a great deal of experience and taught him how to satisfy even the most exacting clients. He works with a team of experienced professionals and coordinates the whole of the construction process: from the structural work to the smallest details of the finish.

He will also help the client to select an architect and work on the basis of plans already drawn up by architects.

Vincent Vangheluwe carries out both new-build and renovation projects according to the wishes of the client. This dialogue with the customer is of prime importance: after all, everything about the building process is based on trust, which is why this experienced and thorough adviser chose the name "Trust" to represent himself and his company.

The photos in this report were taken in Vincent Vangheluwe's discreet townhouse, in the heart of the Flemish Ardennes.

Trust operates as a consultancy for the entire construction process, up to and including the choice of materials and the perfect finish. Only materials of the highest quality are used.

AN OASIS OF SPACE

As with all of its other projects, the Schellen architectural studio created both the architecture and the interior of this contemporary home.

Linda Coart was responsible for the functional and clean design, which extends seamlessly from outside to inside.

The entrance to the house is reached by passing under the suspended beam and taking the wooden path over the large pond. To the left is the carport, concealed behind a wall with a dark 'crépi' finish.

p. 74

Part of the façade is finished in quartz-zinc sections.

On the garden side of the house, large glass sections ensure a perfect connection between inside and outside. The interplay of extensive sheets of glass, freestanding columns, horizontal canopies and vertical sections is a trademark of architect Reginald Schellen. The garden, with its clean lines, is by Tom Caes.

The quartz-zinc makes another appearance as a material for the pool house (created by Ilse Plancke).

The dining room has most contact with the garden because of the beautiful open space with its huge glass section. Curtain frames by Reynaers aluminium ensure a streamlined look. The oak parquet floor has been bleached.

The long gas fire within the black wall dominates the sitting area. There is also a view of the library and multimedia room from here.

The tall wooden sliding door can be used to close off this space.

The kitchen looks out onto the garden. The large covered area is an invitation to eat outside. The unit with the sink and counter is made of stainless steel. All of the kitchen equipment has been combined to form a whole. Enamelled glass has been installed behind the cooking area.

The office at the top of the open space forms a central location with a panoramic view over the beautiful garden.

The Boffi bath with matching basins and fittings is an eye-catching feature in the bathroom. The shower walls have been finished in the same Cotto d'Este tiles that are used in the kitchen and entrance hall.

WARM MINIMALISM

A family with growing teenage daughters exchanged life in the city for the leafy out-skirts, finding a beautifully situated location for construction in the middle of woodland. Architect Michal Muylaert translated the desires of the clients – light, space, peace and a great sense of openness, combined with sufficient privacy for the residents – into a sober, timeless architecture with a blind façade and a glass rear wall that looks out on-to the garden and woods. The spaces flow seamlessly into one another, but ceiling-height doors and sliding partitions can create separate rooms and privacy if needed.

Involving architects and interior designers (Koen Aerts, Pas-Partoe and Kultuz) in the pro-ject right from the beginning has resulted in a great sense of harmony between the colours, materials, light and proportions. This blurs the boundary between inside and out-side and creates a real feeling of space. The whole concept is sober and minimal in de-sign, but has been created in warm, straightforward materials that bring a comfortable atmosphere to the clean lines of the house.

Art is given a prominent position in the spacious entrance hall.

The specially made fireplace wall contains a wide gas fire. A cupboard space for audio and bar has been incorporated almost invisibly into the chimney breast.

Throughout the ground floor there are custom-made concrete tiles that contrast with the simple white walls. The stairs have also been laid with the same tiles.

The open kitchen was designed by the owners of the house as an extension of the living room. The cupboards are in dark-grey stained oak and the surfaces are in lava stone. Cooker-hood filters, indirect lighting and loudspeakers are incorporated into the canopy above the counter.

The furniture was carefully selected and comes mainly from the collections of Minotti and Piet Boon.

Next to the sitting area is a wellness and relaxation space with loungers, a sauna, a Turkish steam bath and a large walk-in shower. Dark, earthy shades ensure a serene, yet cosy, atmosphere.

p. 100-101
The home office with
furniture from Bulo has
large windows onto the
garden, which provide a
wonderful view.

Warm shades create a sense of calm and comfort in the master bedroom, which also connects to the bathroom. The side walls have been left open: the shower, washbasins, toilet and storage space have all been accommodated within a large, central block.

CONTEMPORARY CLASSIC

Interior architect Philip Simoen created the interior of this contemporary classic house designed by architect Marc Verstraeten.

The old staircase has been retained. The floor is laid in Cotto d'Este Buxy tiles. Kreon wall-lighting. The paintwork is by Kordekor.

Flexform seating and a Mario Botta table. Solid-oak parquet on the floor.

The kitchen floor is also laid in Cotto d'Este Buxy tiles. Dresser and table in aged oak veneer. The kitchen is custom-built, with Formica units.
Kitchen equipment by Miele.

The wardrobe and wall behind the bed are in aged oak veneer.

The wardrobes in the dressing room are in painted MDF. There is a solid-oak parquet floor in this space as well.

CONTEMPORARY ART
AND DESIGN IN A MONOCHROME
WHITE INTERIOR

Claire Bataille and Paul ibens, a design duo, devised the interior of this house, which is idyllically situated with a panoramic view of open countryside.

The theme running through this house is the monochrome white in which all of the walls and ceilings are painted. This forms the perfect backdrop for the owner's collection of contemporary art.

The hall floor has been laid with black ceramic tiles of 10x10 cm.

The walls and ceiling have been painted white. Art by Guy Mees (left) and Shapiro (right).

Walls and ceilings have been painted monochrome white here as well, the ideal backdrop for the modern art by Bruce Nauman, Lawrence Weiner, Sol LeWitt and Lauhaus.
The sofa is a design by Claire Bataille & Paul ibens. B&B table and a Poul Kjaerholm pouf.
White chairs designed by Verner Panton.

p. 120-121
In the background are two
Mies van der Rohe chairs
with art by Sena above.
Oak parquet and white
walls and ceilings
throughout.

The table and benches were designed by Claire Bataille and Paul ibens, produced by Feld.

The kitchen floor is in black ceramic tiles.

The bathroom is clad in light-grey Briant.

An oak parquet floor has been laid in the bedroom.

As everywhere else in the house, the walls and ceilings have been painted white.

PLAYING WITH LIGHT AND SPACE

This contemporary house, a compact volume that is entirely focused on the exterior, was created by Baudouin Courtens for an "artist of light".
Light is the theme that runs throughout this house: in both its natural and its artificial forms.

The choice of materials was driven by an urge to use natural elements and shades: brown terracotta roof tiles, copper guttering and drains, lime plasterwork, bluestone and grey windows.

The house is built on a steep slope, the potential of which has been perfectly exploited.

The entrance hall, which forms the distribution axis to the different spaces in this house, is the ideal place to exhibit the owner's art collection. Works by Laurence Demaison and Yves Ullens.

The sitting room forms the heart of the house: it opens onto the garden, the interior spaces (the hall, the music room) and the stairs. A long lava-stone bench provides space for the wrought-iron open fireplace. The music system has been incorporated into the chimney breast.

The colour palette consists of muted shades, contrasting sharply with the explosion of colours in the works by Claire Corey, Jean-Luc Moerman and Yves Ullens.

The staircase and corridor leading to the swimming pool are in the same materials. Art by Liliane Lacasse and Glen Luchford.

The first-floor mezzanine is bathed in light thanks to the open space over two floors in the staircase hallway. A work by Yves Zurstrassen.

The staircase was designed as a sculpture and stands completely free of the walls. The glass on the stairs reinforces the effect of the light.

p. 134

The sloping terrain has made it possible to locate the swimming pool underground, and still maintain a direct connection to the garden.

Floors in treated lava stone. The walls have been rendered with a layer of structured lime-based plaster.

The swimming pool has been lined with anthracite-grey glass mosaic, lending a beautiful depth to the basin.

The main bathroom is designed as a contrast of white and dark brown: polished and bushhammered white Carrara marble and tinted oak furniture.

In the daughter's bedroom, a door has been integrated into a block of wall units, providing a sober entrance to the bathroom.

In the alcove, a bench and a piece by Bruno Bisang.

The master dressing room is designed as an antechamber and is fully panelled in oak.

PART II

LOFTS AND APARTMENTS

A CONTEMPORARY TRANSFORMATION WITH RESPECT FOR THE ORIGINAL

An entire floor (ca. 220 m^2) of an old factory was completely transformed by interior architect Yvonne Hennes to create a contemporary loft. She also took charge of the interior design.
The owner, a young woman, wanted a bright and functional space.

Yvonne Hennes went for sober and timeless furnishings, whilst at the same time leaving the charm of this authentic space intact.

The lift takes you straight into the apartment.

A wall that does not reach the ceiling marks the entrance to the sitting room. This creates a feeling of cosiness, whilst maintaining the sense of space.

The cupboard for coats is suspended from this wall. On the sitting-room side this block contains an old dresser and a B&O music system.

p. 146-147
The floor of the loft is laid with a bleached-oak parquet floor. The sitting-room furniture, the table and the chairs are by Maxalto.

p. 148-149
The kitchen space is part of the living area and was created by Yvonne Hennes. Kitchen units in painted MDF panels.

A sliding door separates the bathroom
from the bedroom.
A contemporary, young and bright
atmosphere.
A stool and chair from the old factory
are a reminder of the origins of this
loft apartment.

CALM AND SERENITY
WITH A VIEW OF THE SEA

Every interior designed by Claire Bataille and Paul ibens emanates a feeling of calm and serenity.

This recent project by the designer duo is a good example of this: the sober, almost monastic design of a seaside apartment in which a key part is played by the collection of modern art.

The art in the hall, which has a dark-brown stone floor, is by Roni Horn.

A painting by Opie above a sofa designed by Christian Liaigre.
The coffee table is a design by Claire Bataille & Paul ibens.

p. 156-157
Two works by
Panamarenko in the
background.
White chairs by Liaigre.
The carpet is from the
Philippines.

The dining-room table is a design by Bataille and ibens.

A view from the hall into the living room and kitchen.

The terrace (at the back in the photo) faces south and allows the light
to flow all the way through to the front of the apartment.

159

Desk chair by Bataille & ibens from Bulo.

The desk was custom-made for this project.

The walls are white throughout and the floor has been laid with dark-grey tinted oak parquet.

A LOFT
IN A FORMER ICE FACTORY

A single woman asked interior architect Bert Van Bogaert to design a loft in this former ice factory: an apartment with limited floor space and a high ceiling.

Within a limited budget, Bert Van Bogaert has succeeded in creating a streamlined and minimalist look that corresponds perfectly to the wishes of the client.

On the left, the tall window sections that allow a great deal of light into the space and provide a view over the garden.

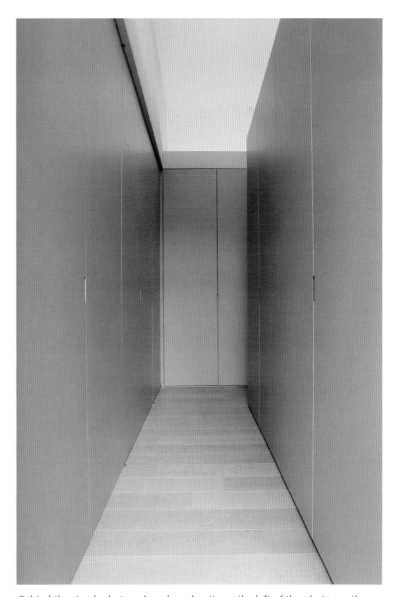

Behind the simply designed cupboard units on the left of the photo are the guest toilet, storage space and technical equipment. To the right is the space for coats and additional storage.

A view of the TV wall and through into the sleeping area.

p. 166-167
A view over the living
space, kitchen and
office.

The sliding panel can be moved from left to right to screen off the kitchen and office. The surfaces in the kitchen and office and the sliding panel are made of solid oak, which has been coloured and given a grey tint.

p. 172-173
The indirect strip lighting gives a warm, atmospheric effect throughout the whole loft, in harmony with the solid oak floor, with its white-grey oiled finish.

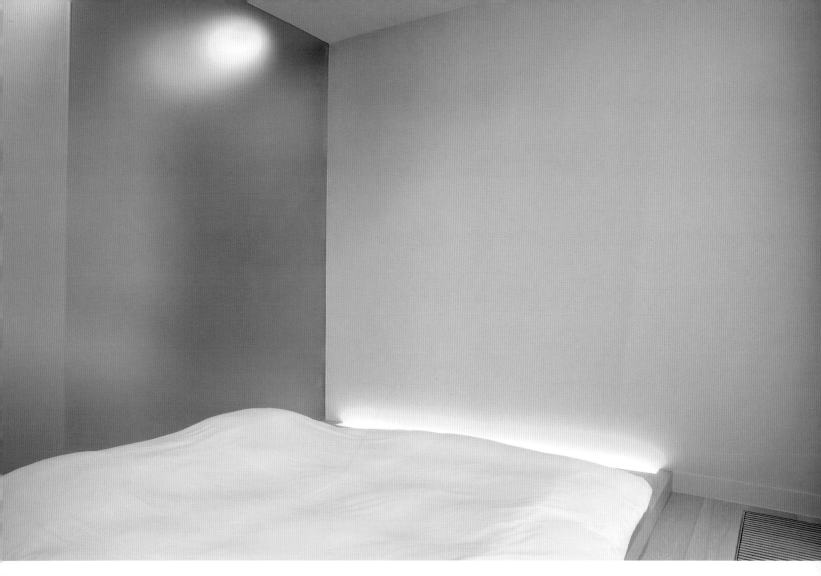

Matt glass separates the bathroom and sleeping area, making it impossible to look through from one space into the other.

p. 174
This interesting view from the bedroom provides direct contact with the living space.

Toning colours in the
tiles and the custom-
made furniture.

Washbasin mounted on
a tiled surface in the
guest toilet.

SPACE FOR MODERN ART

When these clients called upon the services of interior architects Koen Aerts and Bart Van Boom (both were still at Obumex at the time, but now have their own design studio), they had just bought an uncompleted penthouse apartment.

The clients had a great many questions: they wanted to know how this apartment could be made to match the sense of space in their home and how they could give their art collection the place that it deserved. Fortunately, as the structural work had not yet been carried out, the interior architects were able to completely rework the usual stereotypical floor plan according to the specific needs of this art-loving couple.

One bedroom was sacrificed so that a reception room and a TV salon could be created. The classic design of the bedroom area was transformed into a suite flowing through from the bedroom into a luxurious wet room. The open kitchen became the focal point of the design. The bold central unit flows on seamlessly into the sideboard and forms the boundary between the nighttime and daytime areas of the apartment. The colours have deliberately been kept plain and timeless so as to display the works of art to their best advantage.

The furniture was selected by Obumex and includes pieces from the collections of B&B, Maxalto and Liaigre.

Built-in spotlights could not be installed within the prefabricated concrete ceilings. In collaboration with Tekna from Lokeren, custom-made spotlight strips were developed that emphasise the lines of the architecture.

The spacious (over 100m²) terrace provides a beautiful panorama over the city.

The tall cupboard units and parquet are in aged oak. The central kitchen block turns seamlessly into a sideboard in off-white matt lacquer and with French white-stone surfaces (Massangis Clair). All of the custom-made work is by Obumex.

p. 184-185
The ceiling-height oak cupboards by Obumex run through from the living area to become wardrobes in the bedroom, thereby increasing the sense of space.

The same brown Cotto d'Este tiles for floor and ceiling in the wet room, beautifully setting off the freestanding white bath. White-lacquered wooden slatted blinds (via Trendson) filter the light entering the bedroom.

CONTEMPORARY TOTAL INTERIORS TAILORED TO THE CLIENT

Van Ransbeeck Total Interiors is a family concern with over thirty years of experience in the design and creation of custom-made interiors.

The company has its own traditional workshop where skilled cabinet-makers and painters ensure perfect production and finishing from A to Z.

After the clients get in touch, the company pays a visit to gauge their needs and desires. Measurements are taken, if necessary, and then an initial proposal is worked out.

Van Ransbeeck's photo-realistic depictions of their projects are one of the company's trump cards: these ensure that, even during the design phase, the client has a clear picture of how the interior will look.
The company then produces a quote for the work and the schedule is determined.

While the work is being carried out, the client remains in constant contact with Van Ransbeeck, as everything is designed and produced in the company's own workshops.

Whether the project involves a kitchen, a bathroom, a bedroom, a sitting room or a complete interior, you can always rely on Van Ransbeeck for a creative and functional design, professional workmanship and dedicated project coordination.

PUBLISHER

BETA-PLUS Publishing

Termuninck 3

B - 7850 Enghien (Belgium)

T +32 (0)2 395 90 20

F +32 (0)2 395 90 21

www.betaplus.com

betaplus@skynet.be

PHOTOGRAPHY

All pictures: Jo Pauwels, except:

p. 116-125 & 152-161 Jean-Luc Laloux,

and 188-191 N. Van Ransbeeck.

GRAPHIC DESIGN

POLYDEM

Nathalie Binart

TRANSLATION

Laura Watkinson

January 2007

ISBN 13: 978 90 772 1377 3

ISBN 10: 90 772 1377 5

A project by RR Interiors.